GARY PAULSEN

ALL ABOUT THE AUTHOR™

GARY PAULSEN

DENIS E. McGUINNESS AND SARAH L. THOMSON

ROSEN PUBLISHING®
New York

Published in 2016 by The Rosen Publishing Group, Inc.
29 East 21st Street, New York, NY 10010

First Edition

Library of Congress Cataloging-in-Publication Data

McGuinness, Denis E.
Gary Paulsen / Denis E. McGuinness and Sarah L. Thomson. -- First edition.
pages cm. -- (All about the author)
Includes bibliographical references and index.
ISBN 978-1-4994-6268-5 (library bound)
1. Paulsen, Gary. 2. Authors, American--20th century--Biography--Juvenile literature. 3. Adventure and adventurers--United States--Biography--Juvenile literature. 4. Young adult fiction--Authorship--Juvenile literature. I. Thomson, Sarah L. II. Title.
PS3566.A834Z78 2016
813'.54--dc23
[B]

2015020298

Manufactured in China

CONTENTS

INTRODUCTION 6

CHAPTER ONE ON HIS OWN 10

CHAPTER TWO LIFE IN THE PHILIPPINES 18

CHAPTER THREE ESCAPING LIFE'S DIFFICULTIES 27

CHAPTER FOUR ALWAYS A REBEL 37

CHAPTER FIVE RUNNING DOGS 46

CHAPTER SIX THE IDITAROD 54

CHAPTER SEVEN JUMP-STARTING A CAREER 63

CHAPTER EIGHT "TO SEEK A BEGINNING" 77

FACT SHEET ON GARY PAULSEN 85

FACT SHEET ON GARY PAULSEN'S WORK 86

CRITICAL REVIEWS 92

TIMELINE 95

GLOSSARY 97

FOR MORE INFORMATION 99

FOR FURTHER READING 102

BIBLIOGRAPHY 103

INDEX 109

INTRODUCTION

Most of the stories that Gary Paulsen writes are based on incidents in his own life. Paulsen is particularly well known as the author of suspenseful adventure stories, in which his young main characters struggle to survive on their own in the natural world. Thirteen-year-old Brian Robeson, the main character of *Hatchet* and four other books, is stranded by a plane crash in the Canadian woods. Russel, of *Dogsong* (like *Hatchet*, a Newbery Honor book), runs a team of sled dogs through the Alaskan wilderness. David Alspeth rides out a storm at sea in *The Voyage of the Frog.*

Although to most readers Paulsen is best known for his survival stories, his other works touch on different aspects of his own adventurous and often difficult life. Events from his childhood visits with relatives on Minnesota farms are retold in such novels as *The Winter Room*, his third Newbery Honor book, *Harris and Me*, and *Family Ties: The Theory, Practice, and Destructive Properties of Relatives*. His relationship with his gentle, nurturing grandmother gave rise to *The Cookcamp*, *Alida's Song*, and *The Quilt.* Memories of a summer when he ran away from home, hoed beets with immigrant laborers, and worked at a carnival later shaped two works, the novel *Tiltawhirl John* and a memoir, *The Beet Fields*. In *How Angel Peterson Got His Name: And Other Outrageous Tales About Extreme*

Gary Paulsen pets Flax, an Alaskan husky, while preparing for the Iditarod. Paulsen has written adventure books in which he has incorporated his own experiences with nature, dogs, and sailing.

Sports, Paulsen relates how he and his friends tried to wrestle a bear, shoot waterfalls in a pickle barrel, and break the speed record for snow skiing in Minnesota, among other daring adventures during the mid-1950s.

In 2010, Paulsen wrote *Woods Runner*, a historical novel about Samuel, a teenager who lived during the Revolutionary War. The story involves Samuel's journey to New York City to try to find his parents, who have been taken prisoner by British soldiers. Although the book is another survival story, Paulsen researched and studied the history, as he had enjoyed doing in the writing of his previous books *Nightjohn* and *Soldier's Heart.*

Most of Paulsen's life has been lived close to the natural world—hunting, fishing, trapping, sailing, and running a team of sled dogs. This connection to nature has meant a life filled with danger. Often, Paulsen has been close to death and barely managed to save himself. Sometimes, when he wasn't able to save himself, he had to be helped. That help didn't always come from other people. It sometimes came from the team of sled dogs that took him through the Alaskan wilderness. Paulsen even returned the favor once by saving his sled dogs after an accident while training for his second attempt at the Iditarod, a grueling dogsled race. In the winter of 1984–85, he, his dogs, and sled fell down the face of a mountain during a blizzard.

Paulsen was able to save his dogs. He saved them

because he thought of them not as pets or as working animals, who were somehow his possessions, but as a team of which they were all a part. Through years of living in intimate contact with nature, Gary Paulsen had come to realize that he was not separate from his dogs, or from other animals, or from any part of the natural world. This understanding changed the way he lived—he stopped hunting and trapping animals. It also shaped the books that he wrote, in which characters such as Brian Robeson of *Hatchet* find that they must not conquer the natural world, but rather become a part of it and listen to what it has to teach them. Only then can an individual survive.

On his official website (http://www.garypaulsen.com), Paulsen has said that it is his "overwhelming belief in young people that drives him to write." He wants to draw on the human spirit and to inspire readers to look about them—at their environment—and treasure their natural surroundings. He has written nearly two hundred books for young people and adults and he continues to read letters from his fans (sometimes up to four hundred letters each day). According to a live chat with Paulsen in 2003 at the New York Public Library, he often tells young adult readers to read "like a wolf eats, read when they tell you not to read, and read what they tell you not to read. Read all the time, and turn the television off. Drive a stake through its heart."

CHAPTER ONE

ON HIS OWN

Gary Paulsen is often admired as the author of compelling young adult fiction that is set in the wilderness. His books for young adults focus on teenagers who come to understand their own character and feelings through their personal and complex experiences with nature. It is through these experiences that they rise to their challenges and survive. Gary Paulsen was also changed by his contact with nature and found comfort in the wilderness, despite his near-death experiencess.

BIRTH AND EARLY CHILDHOOD

Gary Paulsen was born on May 17, 1939, in Minneapolis, Minnesota. His father, Oscar Paulsen, was an army officer stationed there when he met Gary's mother, Eunice Moen. Shortly after Gary's birth, Oscar Paulsen was called to fight in World War II. He spent most of the war in Europe. Gary was much too young to remember his father and would not see him again for seven years. Gary's mother moved with her son to Chicago, Illinois, in 1944, when Gary was four. She took a job at a munitions factory (where weapons for the war effort were built), leaving Gary in the care of a woman named Clara. Clara's "care" was

A woman assembles a motor at an airplane factory in 1942. During World War II, Gary's mother worked in a weapons factory in Chicago, Illinois, and had to leave Gary in the care of another woman while she was at her job.

not particularly thorough; she drank red wine out of jelly jars, listened to the radio, and mostly ignored the young child she was supposed to be watching.

Even when his mother was home from work, Gary was not closely supervised. One weekend while his mother was taking a nap, young Gary slipped outside to play in a nearby alley. Suddenly, he was grabbed by a man—filthy, smelling of alcohol, urine, and vomit—who lifted the terrified child up off the ground. Gary was too frightened and shocked to struggle, and he would likely have been molested by this man if his mother had not appeared. She attacked the man, hitting him in the head until he dropped Gary, then knocking him down and kicking him with her heavy, steel-toed work shoes until he lay still—perhaps dead.

When she saw a threat to her son, Gary's mother was savagely protective. Once, when Gary was very young and in the hospital with pneumonia, the doctors believed that he would not live. They called in a priest to give him last rites. But when Gary's mother saw the priest—who to her suggested death—she could not stand the thought that her son might die. Furious, she shouted at him and drove him from the room, as if her anger would be enough to keep her child alive. She attacked Gary's would-be molester with the same kind of rage.

One night Gary woke up to hear his mother crying. She told him that she was lonely and that his father had a "friend" where he was stationed in France. She would often come home late, with alcohol on her breath, and on weekends took the four-year-old Gary to bars with her.

Soon, Gary's mother had a "friend" of her own, a man named Casey. Casey moved in with Eunice and Gary and stayed until the end of the war. During Casey's first year with the family, Gary was sent to spend the summer with his grandmother, who worked as a cook for a work crew cutting a road through the Minnesota woods. The nurturing warmth of Gary's grandmother and the affection of the tough working men who adopted the little boy are retold in Paulsen's novel *The Cookcamp*. But at the end of the summer, Gary returned to the uncomfortable situation of living with his mother and "Uncle Casey."

At last, in 1945, World War II was over. Gary, now six years old, thought this meant that Casey would finally leave and his father would come home. And Casey did indeed move out, but Gary's father did not come back. Instead, he was reassigned to the Philippines.

NO EASY TRIP

In 1946, Gary's mother managed to get both herself and her son to San Francisco, where they were to catch a troopship to the Philippines. But along the way, Gary caught chicken pox. He would not have been able to pass the medical exam required to leave the country, but Gary's mother convinced the ship's captain to help them. The seven-year-old boy was smuggled onto the troopship and left alone in a

The USS *West Point*, a troopship, is docked at port in 1944. Gary and his mother rode a troopship from San Francisco, California, to Manila, in the Philippines, in 1946 to join his father, who had been reassigned to a military base there.

cabin overnight, until his mother came on board the next morning. The ship set sail, but Gary had to stay in the dispensary, where sailors came for medical treatment. He was there for nine days. A corpsman (or medic) named Harding looked after him while he was in the dispensary, bringing him food and reading comic books to him.

OSCAR PAULSEN

Gary's father, Oscar, was a decorated soldier who served on General George Patton's staff. Gary once said about his early years, "I was an 'army brat,' and it was a miserable life." Gary's father had worked his way up the ranks to major and had fought in Europe and Africa. Gary had often thought about what it would be like to meet him, dreaming of a father who would scoop him up in his arms, who would have gifts and toys for him. But when the time came, Gary found that he was shy, almost frightened. His father promised that they would have plenty of time to get to know each other. "And because I was young and didn't know any better," Gary Paulsen wrote in *Eastern Sun, Winter Moon* (1993), "I believed him."

A HORRIFIC SCENE

The first time Gary was allowed out of the cabin should have been exciting—he was to see the sky for the first time in more than a week and the ocean for the first time in his life. But instead, it was horrifying. As his mother brought Gary up on deck, a plane crashed into the ocean near the ship. Gary watched as the plane hit the surface and broke in half. Survivors spilled into the water and climbed out onto the wings. Some were hurt and bleeding. Gary would learn later that the people on the plane were the wives and children of soldiers coming back to the mainland United States from Hawaii.

Much later, when Paulsen was writing *Hatchet*, he remembered this crash, especially the jolt of the plane striking water that seemed as solid as cement because of the aircraft's speed when it hit.

Boats from the troopship set out at once to rescue the survivors, and it seemed that everything might be all right. But then sharks attacked. These sharks had been following the ship for miles, eating the garbage that was thrown overboard. They smelled the blood of the injured people and attacked the survivors who fell or jumped into the water to get away from the sinking plane. Horrified, Gary watched as people died in the water before the boats could reach them.

After the injured survivors were brought onto the troopship, Gary's mother helped the corpsman, Harding, take care of them. Several children had been on board the plane with their mothers. One, a little boy no bigger than Gary, died on the deck as Gary watched. When Gary made his way down to the dispensary, where he had been staying, he found it full of survivors needing care. Looking around for his beloved stuffed animal, Dog, Gary spotted him at last—held tightly in the arms of an injured little girl. Gary decided to let her keep the toy.

As the ship changed course and headed for Hawaii, Gary made friends with a boy named Jimmy, whose mother had been killed in the crash. Jimmy never spoke except to swear at the sharks that were still following the ship, but together he and Gary explored the troopship from top to bottom. After taking Jimmy and the other survivors back to Hawaii, the ship resumed its original course, and eventually Gary and his mother reached the Philippines. At last, when he was seven years old, Gary met his father. His long-awaited meeting with his father was a huge letdown.

CHAPTER TWO

LIFE IN THE PHILIPPINES

When Gary arrived in Manila, the capital of the Philippines, little did he know that life with his parents would soon disintegrate into not only the horrors of war but also the terrors of alcoholism. The Philippines had been occupied by the Japanese army during World War II and retaken by the Allies in 1945. The fighting had devastated the country. From the dock where the ship landed, Gary could see the signs of war: rubble in the streets, a building with the windows and floors blown away, craters in the road big enough to hold a truck. And the violence was not over. There was still fighting going on between a guerrilla group and the American military. The guerrillas, called Huks, wanted the government to

An American bombing mission liberated Manila from Japanese occupation in 1945. When Gary and his mother landed in Manila the following year, many of the city streets and buildings were still in ruins.

divide the estates of wealthy landowners among the poor.

A NEW HOME

Gary's new home was on a military compound near Manila. He would live there for the next three years. Unfortunately, Gary's hope of getting to know his father wasn't to be fulfilled. Oscar Paulsen was busy with work, and he rarely spoke to his son except to give orders or to tell him rules. Gary's mother was quickly caught up in the social activities of an officer's wife—playing cards, having tea parties, going to ladies' nights at the officers' club. But there was a worse problem, one that was to take Gary's parents away from him in a deeper way. Both of them were drinking heavily. Gary rarely saw them, and when he did, they were usually drunk.

Once again, Gary was on his own. There was a school on the military base, but because there were so few children and because fighting was still going on, classes were often canceled. Gary had plenty of time to explore, and he soon became bored with the usual activities near his home: watching the monkey the neighbors kept chained up in the backyard, watching the trucks driving by, and playing inside the rusty remains of a bombed-out Japanese tank.

There were no other children nearby, but Gary did have a companion. Rom was one of the two Filipino servants Gary's father had hired to help run the household. He made time to play with Gary and found a bicycle to take him for rides around the compound. They watched planes at the airstrip and rode to the exchange (a military-run store) to buy cups of warm Coca-Cola. Rom took him to play inside a downed Japanese airplane.

A cargo ship unloads supplies at the army base in Manila. Gary felt rather lonely on the base—not many children attended the base's school and it was challenging to find friends.

But Gary soon grew restless and wanted a wider world to explore. His father had forbidden him to go outside the military compound; he might have been kidnapped by the guerrillas. But Gary found a way to get around his father's restriction.

A WAY OUT

One day, Gary caught Rom stealing two cans of sardines from the kitchen. There were almost no jobs in the Philippines at that time, and most people were desperately poor. Rom needed the food to feed his family. But if Gary told on him, Rom would be fired. It would be almost impossible for him to find another job. His family might starve. From that time on, Rom did anything that Gary wanted. And what Gary wanted was to go outside the compound.

During their first time outside the base, Rom saw a boy working with water buffalo in a rice paddy and arranged for Gary to ride on the buffalo's back. On later trips, they visited Rom's family in their two-room shack and ate rice and sardines with them. Gary learned to like *baloots*, a Filipino delicacy that consisted of duck eggs allowed to sit in hot sand until the body of the unhatched duckling inside had partially rotted. He found them especially good when washed down with warm Coca-Cola.

Gary questioned Rom about the war and the Japanese occupation. When Rom told him about a nearby cave filled with the corpses of Japanese soldiers, Gary insisted on going to see it. The entrance to the cave was blocked with dirt, but Gary saw a small hole and before Rom could stop him, he scrambled inside. There were skeletons inside, clad in rotting uniforms. But even worse, there were rats that had grown huge from feasting on the dead bodies. Panicked, Gary screamed for Rom, who came to

GARY AND DOGS

Although Snowball was Gary's first dog, he would have many dogs as pets throughout his life. Dogs taught him a different way of looking at his surroundings. During a live chat at the New York Public Library in 2003, Paulsen said, "Sled dogs . . . kind of took over and raised me. I love dogs. They are God's gift." Over the years, Paulsen has owned border collies, a basset hound, Chihuahuas, various breeds of sled dogs, and hunting dogs.

get him and brought him back outside into the sunlight. Rom waited patiently until Gary stopped crying. Afterward, they never spoke of the cave again.

SNOWBALL

During his first year in the Philippines, Gary found a second companion. Her name was Snowball, and she was his first dog. In the Philippines, it was common for people to eat dogs, and Snowball was destined for the cooking pot before Gary saw her and begged his mother to save her. Once Gary's mother bought the puppy, Snowball and Gary became inseparable. Snowball was the first of many dogs in his life to teach Gary a new way of looking at the world, using every sense to discover as much as possible about his surroundings. "I would see things," Paulsen recalled in *My Life in Dog Years* (1998), "blown-apart buildings, old tanks, Jeeps upside down, rusting guns everywhere—but Snowball would *know* things. She would see the obvious outside way a thing looked, but then she would move to it and smell it and perhaps lick it and dig at it and look under it and I took to doing the same things."

Following Snowball's lead, Gary became more aware of everything around him. Not aware enough, however, to notice a snake near his bare foot before Snowball leaped at it and killed it. Later, he would learn that this type of snake was deadly. Snowball had saved his life.

During the years that Gary spent in the Philippines with Snowball and Rom as his companions, he grew more and more detached from his parents. One of the few events he did share with his mother and father was a trip to a nearby island. Gary's father had arranged a canoe trip down a river to a scenic lake. While the adults ate a picnic, Gary, who couldn't swim, played in the shallows.

Everything would have been fine, except that Gary found a log to float on and was soon washed into violent rapids where the river flowed out of the lake. He would have drowned if a young Filipino boy had not grabbed him and pulled him out of the water. Gary's mother held her son tightly, shaken at the near loss, and then pulled him back into the lake, dragging him by the hand as he struggled against her. She insisted that if he didn't go in the water then, he'd be afraid of it for the rest of his life. Fully clothed, she knelt down and played with him in the shallow water until he was no longer afraid.

This was one of the few times Gary felt connected to either of his parents. He wrote in *Eastern Sun, Winter Moon* that he didn't want to see them—they both were becoming strangers to him, almost always drunk and always fighting.

Snowball was a more reliable friend. Gary would talk to her about the problems in his life and she seemed to understand. Sadly, just two weeks before Gary and his family were to return to the United States, Snowball was hit by a truck while she and Gary were walking by the side of the road. "I remember standing, not believing she was dead," Paulsen wrote in *My Life in Dog Years*, "thinking how nothing would ever be right again, not ever, and how I would always, always miss her."

After three years in the Philippines, in 1949, Gary and his mother returned to the United States. His

Oscar Paulsen, Gary's father, completed his military service with the army at the newly finished Pentagon, in Washington, D.C. Afterward, the Paulsens moved to Thief River Falls, in Minnesota, where they tried to find work.

father followed shortly afterward. They spent nine months in Washington, D.C., while Gary's father finished his military service at the Pentagon, the building of which had been completed in 1943. The Paulsens then moved back to Minnesota, to Thief River Falls, which was chiefly an agricultural town in the northwestern part of the state. It is located about 70 miles (113 kilometers) south of the Canadian border.

CHAPTER THREE

ESCAPING LIFE'S DIFFICULTIES

Gary's parents' problems with alcohol continued. It seemed as if they did nothing but drink and fight. When the family first moved back to Minnesota, Gary's father made an attempt to raise chickens for a living. When that did not work out, Oscar Paulsen tried his hand at other kinds of employment to supplement his military pension—tending bar, managing a liquor store, working in a gas station. But his jobs rarely lasted for long, and the family had little money. "I was one of the wasted ones," Gary Paulsen wrote in a memoir *Father Water, Mother Woods*, about the years he spent with his family in Minnesota. "One of the emotionally injured, who awakened crying in the night, the boys who saw with wide eyes and could say nothing."

School wasn't much better than home. Because the family was constantly moving while Gary's father tried new jobs, the longest time Gary spent in any single school was five months. He tried to fit in, but failed at almost everything. He once wrote, "School was a nightmare because I was unbelievably shy, and terrible at sports."

MAKING EXTRA MONEY

From the age of thirteen or fourteen on, Gary worked as many jobs as he could, trying to earn enough for spending money and school clothes. He sold newspapers in bars, waiting until late so that his customers would be drunk enough to pay a little more. He set pins in a bowling alley until 11:30 p.m. on weeknights. He spent summers working on farms, doing backbreaking agricultural labor all day long for as little as two dollars and his meals. The summer he was sixteen, Gary ran away from home for a time. He headed west, to North Dakota, where he ended up working alongside migrant workers from Mexico, something he described in *The Beet Fields* (2000). He told of the arduous work on the beet farm, where the farmer charged the laborers for the use of hoes, living quarters, and for the tasteless sandwiches that

Migrant workers toil in beet fields in California. Gary did grueling work alongside migrant laborers in the beet fields of North Dakota during the summer after he ran away from home. He characterized the experience in his book *The Beet Fields*.

served as the only food at hand. As a result, the laborers were left a paltry sum as their wages.

LIVING WITH HIS MATERNAL RELATIVES

Running away from home was only one of the ways Gary tried to escape the difficulties of his life. When things got particularly bad with his parents, he would stay with his mother's relatives. He spent his eleventh summer with his mother's cousin and his family, a time that later became the basis for the novel *Harris and Me*. His experiences of farm life with his relatives helped shape his Newbery Honor novel *The Winter Room*, which is a tribute to the power of land and family, memory, and storytelling. In *The Winter Room*, he wrote that in the winter, every evening began in the same way, "Uncle David and Nels will fill their lower lips [with tobacco] and Father will carve and Mother will knit and the yellow flames will make our faces burn…Uncle David will spit in the coffee can …and take a breath and say 'It was when I was young…"

Sadly, the visits to relatives always eventually ended, and Gary would have to go home.

A PIVOTAL EVENT

After a while, to steer clear of his parents, he moved into the basement of his family's apartment building. He found an alcove behind the furnace with an old couch and a lightbulb hanging from the ceiling and began to spend most of his time there. His parents didn't notice that he had more or less moved out.

Another escape opened up unexpectedly one cold night when Gary was fourteen. He was selling

The philanthropist Andrew Carnegie gave Thief River Falls money to build a public library, which was dedicated in 1915. This library is the one in which Gary sought shelter from the freezing cold and where he obtained his first library card.

newspapers, and, noticing that the library was open, he wandered in to warm up. To his surprise, the librarian asked if he would like a library card. "So she gave me a card, with my name on it," he remembered, according to Leonard S. Marcus, editor of *Author Talk*, "and—God!—it was astonishing what happened to me. It was as though I suddenly had an identity: I was a person."

It took Gary about a month to read the first book the librarian found for him. When he brought it back, she gave him another book. Soon he was reading two or three books every week. "It was as though I had been dying of thirst and the librarian had handed me a five-gallon bucket of water," he said in editor Alan Hedblad's *Something About the Author*. "I drank and drank."

JOINING A CARNIVAL

At the age of fifteen, Gary joined a carnival for a time, and traveled with the carnies, as the people who work with a carnival are known. In his novel *The Beet Fields: Memories of a Sixteenth Summer* (2002), Paulsen tells the story of a sixteen-year-old boy who works long and hard in the fields of a beet farm beside migrant laborers. He then runs away and joins a carnival. At the carnival, the boy runs one of the amusement rides and begins to see the world as a hard and disenchanting place. He learns the typical carny scams, becomes a shill, or promoter, for a "wild man" from Borneo in a sideshow, and meets a girl, Ruby. Paulsen drew on his own experiences in writing many of the details about the life of a roustabout.

FINDING A FRIEND

When Gary was fifteen, he met a man who helped him deal with the struggles of life with alcoholic parents. J. D. was a police officer, and Paulsen, in his *Pilgrimage on a Steel Ride: A Memoir About Men and Motorcycles* (1997), calls him "the primary reason I did not wind up in prison." J. D. caught Gary trying to break into a garage. He didn't take the boy to jail or home to his parents. Instead, he drove Gary out of town and made him walk the six or seven miles (10–11 km) back in freezing, mid-January weather while J. D. followed along in his car. When Gary said he was sure he wasn't going to break into any more garages, J. D. drove him to a diner for a meal.

For two years, Gary spent almost every night in J. D.'s squad car. J. D. was a tough man with little patience for people he didn't like. He was known to hit suspects he had arrested (as long as they were men; it was against J. D.'s principles to hit a woman or a child), and he took violent revenge on people he believed had insulted or injured him.

But he could also be protective, and for reasons Gary never quite understood, he saw something worthwhile in the rebellious teenager who was the son of the town drunks. J. D. helped Gary learn to stand up for himself.

COMFORT IN THE WOODS

In the end, however, it wasn't J. D. or the librarian or his mother's relatives who did the most to help Gary survive his teenage years. The woods were Gary's best refuge. "I ran to the woods and rivers of northern Minnesota," Paulsen wrote of himself and his friends in *Father Water, Mother Woods*, "It was, I suppose, a kind of self-fostering—perhaps a subconscious seeking of help from nature … When we were in the woods or fishing … our lives didn't hurt."

There were other boys like him who needed the money and food that hunting and fishing could bring.

Minnesota's Boundary Waters, in the northern part of the state, are acclaimed for their natural beauty. Gary often retreated to the woods of northern Minnesota to find comfort.

Gary's parents could not always be relied on to keep the kitchen stocked with food or give him the money he needed to buy it. When he didn't eat the fish and game he caught, he sold it to pay for clothes, school or hunting supplies, or hamburgers and milkshakes. After school, on weekends, and on the days he simply chose not to go to school, Gary fished at the local dam and, with a spear or bow, in the drainage ditches—the same way Brian Robeson would catch fish in *Hatchet*. Gary and his friends hunted for grouse, deer, beaver, or rabbits. As he wrote in *Father Water, Mother Woods*, they hunted simply to be outside, where there was beauty everywhere.

"Hunting virtually became my life," Paulsen wrote in *Guts* (2001). He had spent so much time in the woods that when he was fourteen, he was able to track a deer for two days. One night, he finally got close enough to the animal to touch it. But when he told his classmates about his achievement, hoping to impress them, no one believed him.

An uncle gave Gary his first rifle. He would pack matches, bread, salt, and an old aluminum pot, and spend his weekends in the woods. After a while, he came to prefer a bow to the rifle. Although hunting with a bow is much more of a challenge, it forced Gary to pay closer attention to his surroundings. "Hunting with a bow changes all things, even the way to move," he remembered in *Father Water,*

Mother Woods. He said that to get close to the animals you had to be able to observe them to really get to know them.

Just as Brian would do in *Hatchet*, Gary made his own arrows—although Brian had to cut his own arrow shafts and Gary got his from a mail-order catalog. Similar to Brian, after endless practice, Gary learned to look into the absolute center of the target and send the arrow directly there. Hunting with a bow was not easy. Once Gary shot ten arrows at a grouse not ten feet (3.1 m) away, missing every single time. The bird sat still as Gary crawled forward, hoping he could retrieve an arrow. The grouse didn't move until Gary was close enough to touch it, and then it exploded into flight, right in Gary's face.

After many attempts, Gary—just as Brian would do in *Hatchet*—killed his first deer with an arrow. At first the doe hardly seemed to react, and Gary believed that he had missed her—until he saw his arrow in the grass, covered from point to feathers in blood. The doe walked a few steps away, settled down in the grass, and died. As he wrote in *Father Water, Mother Woods*, Gary knew that in a millisecond he had put an end to a magnificent creature, an animal who would never breathe again, and stopped her world forever. Gary never forgot this incident.

CHAPTER FOUR

ALWAYS A REBEL

Despite his struggles in high school (including flunking the ninth grade), Paulsen eventually graduated. He was accepted at Bemidji Teacher's College in Bemidji, Minnesota, where he took preengineering courses. But before he'd been there a year, he failed his courses and flunked out.

THE ARMY

At age seventeen, Gary Paulsen enlisted in the army (he forged his father's signature)—and spent, he wrote in *Winterdance: The Fine Madness of Running the Iditarod*, "three years, eight months, twenty-one days, and nine hours regretting it." He was sent to Colorado for basic training. Taking orders didn't come naturally to Paulsen; "I was a rebel," he was later said to have declared in Gary M. Salvner's *Presenting Gary Paulsen*.

But his drill instructor, Sergeant Gross, immediately challenged his defiant attitude. Gross didn't just punish Paulsen for stepping out of line, he also insisted that the young soldier was wasting his potential and encouraged him to become certified as a field engineer.

When Paulsen was finally discharged from the army in 1962 (he had attained the rank of sergeant) he was not in good emotional shape. "I did not think I could salvage the time I had just wasted, or that I could save my ruined life," he wrote in a memoir, *Caught by the Sea: My Life on Boats* (2001).

BACK TO THE WILDERNESS

As he had done when he was younger, Paulsen turned to the wilderness. But this time it wasn't the woods of Minnesota. It was the sea. He drove from El Paso, Texas, straight to the California coast and spent six days and nights alone by the water. "I walked until I could see the water coming in, rolling in from the vastness," he wrote in *Caught by the Sea*, "and I sat down and let the sea heal me."

TRACKING SATELLITES

Despite Paulsen's distaste for the army, it was the training he'd received there that kept him employed

Paulsen worked at the Goldstone Deep Space Tracking Center in the Mojave Desert in California during the early 1960s. It was while at the center that Paulsen got the idea to become a writer.

for the next three years. With his engineering experience, Paulsen was able to get jobs at aerospace companies. While he was working for the Goldstone Deep Space Tracking Center in California, he read a magazine article on the flight-testing of a new airplane. The article changed his life. Reading had been important to Paulsen since he was a teenager, but now, for the first time, he realized that a person, someone like the author of the article he was reading,

PAULSEN'S AEROSPACE EXPERIENCES

Paulsen used some of his aerospace experiences tracking satellites in the California and New Mexico deserts to write a satire about various problems during the early days of the U.S. missile program. *Some Birds Don't Fly* (1968), Paulsen's first solo book, is a humorous look at some of the early experiments and tests done on rockets, or birds, as they are called in the book, and the missile industry.

could actually make a living as a writer. He quit his job that night, dropped his company car off at a gas station, and left town for Hollywood, determined to learn to write.

BECOMING A WRITER

Paulsen knew nothing about writing, and he thought that the best way to learn would be to edit. After typing up a fairly creative résumé, he got a job at a men's magazine. It turned out that Paulsen had been right—editing was an excellent way to learn to write. "Editing taught me to get to the point with words," he told Leonard Marcus in *Author Talk*. "And it taught me that writing isn't about ego but about getting the words right." Paulsen would spend time at the magazine during the day and go home at night to work on his own writing. The next day, he would bring in whatever he had been working on and his colleagues at the magazine would critique his work. Then Paulsen would go home to write some more. With Raymond Friday Locke, he compiled and wrote *The Special War*, a memoir of his army experiences in Vietnam, which was published in 1966.

Writing was not the only thing Paulsen learned to do in Hollywood. He found work as a film extra and even played a drunken American Indian in the movie *Flap* (1970). He took up wood carving and sculpting as a hobby.

SAILING

He also had his first encounter with something that would become a lifelong obsession: boats. Just as he had gotten a magazine job without having any idea of how to write or edit, Paulsen bought a boat, got on board, began to figure out how to sail—and promptly fell overboard.

In *Caught by the Sea*, Paulsen would call his first sailing trip "a series of calamities punctuated by terror." In the harbor at Ventura, California, he decided to take the boat out to open water. But the instant he got the mainsail up, the wind took the boat off so quickly that Paulsen was dumped over the side and watched his new boat sail off without him. Fortunately, it didn't go far before hitting the rocky shoreline, narrowly missing another boat. Paulsen swam over, climbed aboard, and got the boat headed back toward the mouth of the harbor. On the way, he hit the boat that his sailboat—sailing without him—had missed earlier. He ran into two other boats by the end of that day and still didn't make it out of the harbor.

The southern California coast at Ventura became the site of Paulsen's first sailing expedition. After initially falling overboard on the first day, he was able to regain control of the boat but never made it out of the harbor.

Paulsen slept on the boat that night and woke up as the tide turned. The moonlit night was so beautiful he couldn't stand to waste it sleeping. He took his boat out into the open sea and sailed until dawn, when the wind died, leaving him stranded twelve miles (19.3 km) offshore. Paulsen knew so little about the sea that he didn't notice the growing swells or the wind picking up. He didn't notice that the seabirds had all gone to the sheltered side of nearby islands to ride out the storm they knew was coming. In fact, he didn't realize that he was in any danger until a blast of wind knocked the boat sideways.

The boat stayed on its side, held down by the weight of the sails, while waves threatened to sweep Paulsen out of the cockpit. Tying a rope around his chest, he crawled out onto the deck, hanging on to whatever he could, and managed to drag down both sails, which brought the boat more or less right side up in the water. Somehow, the boat seemed able to keep itself upright. Exhausted, Paulsen stumbled below and promptly fell asleep—only to be woken by a huge wave that slammed down on the boat and filled the cabin with water. He had forgotten to put the boards in place that would close off the interior of the vessel and keep it dry. Paulsen pumped the water out, put up the boards, and fell asleep again. He woke up hours later to a bright, sunny morning.

Although he didn't know it, Paulsen had been blown about 100 miles (161 km) down the coast of California, and he was now caught in a current that would eventually take him another 150 miles (241 km) south. Nevertheless, he finally managed to get back home, learning to sail his new boat along the way.

However, despite his pleasure in sailing, Paulsen was finding it hard to concentrate on his writing in Hollywood.

RETURN TO MINNESOTA

In the late 1960s, he moved to a small cabin in Minnesota, for which he paid twenty-five dollars a week in rent. There he worked as a trapper and hunter while writing. In 1968, his work of nonfiction for adults, *Some Birds Don't Fly*, was published by Rand McNally. The book is a humorous look at the rocket program during its early years and some of the things that happened during experiments and test flights. It was followed shortly afterward by his first book for younger readers, *Mr. Tucket*, published by a company called Funk & Wagnalls, in 1968.

Mr. Tucket is an adventure novel about a boy, fourteen years old, who is kidnapped from his wagon train by a Cheyenne raiding party and rescued by a mountain man, Mr. Grimes. The book didn't earn a lot of critical acclaim. In *Presenting*

A wagon train rolls slowly through a mountainous trail. Paulsen's book *Mr. Tucket* takes place on the Oregon Trail, where Francis, a teen, is kidnapped by Pawnees and later rescued by a one-armed mountain man, Jason Grimes.

Gary Paulsen, Salvner admitted that *Mr. Tucket* is "a cliché-filled and predictable Western, certainly not one of Gary Paulsen's better works." But even with its flaws, *Mr. Tucket* was Gary Paulsen's first step toward a lifelong career of writing for young adults. In 2003, during a live chat at the New York Public Library, an interviewer asked "What made you get into writing for young people?" Paulsen replied, "It is the only place where you can be artistic and have it accepted. To do experimental work and try to do new things with writing."

CHAPTER FIVE

RUNNING DOGS

With the publication of his first two books, Paulsen's writing career seemed set to take off. He moved to Taos, New Mexico, and settled down to work as a writer. But a problem interfered. As both of his parents had done, Paulsen began to drink too much. For the next six years, he struggled with a serious alcohol problem. In addition, to complicate matters, he wasn't able to sell another book. Instead, he worked construction and demolition jobs to make ends meet.

A NEW FAMILY

One good thing did come of his years in Taos: Paulsen met Ruth Ellen Wright. Wright was an artist and former art teacher, and she and Paulsen were married on May 5, 1971. Their son, Jim, was born that same year. Paulsen had been married and divorced twice before, including once while he was in the army, a marriage that ended when Paulsen made his sudden decision to move to California and become a writer. His second brief marriage took place while he lived in Hollywood. Paulsen had two children, Lynn and Lance, with his first wife, but he lost touch with them "through [his] own stupidity," as he later admitted in an interview with Maryann N. Weidt in *Children's Literature Review*; both children were adopted by their mother's second husband. Gary and Ruth are still married.

Finally, in 1973, with the help of Alcoholics Anonymous, Paulsen was able to quit drinking for good. But it took him two years to sell another book. *The Building a New, Buying an Old, Remodeling a Used, Comprehensive Home and Shelter How-to-Do-It Book* was published in 1976. A year later, his young adult novel *Winterkill* was also published. It seemed as if Paulsen's life might be back on track at last. But in 1979, he was sued for libel by a man who thought he recognized himself as one of the characters in *Winterkill*. The lawsuit was eventually dismissed, but the experience left Paulsen so bitter and angry that he almost gave up writing entirely.

Financially, life was a struggle, especially now that Paulsen had a family to support. Finally, in

RUTH WRIGHT PAULSEN

Paulsen's third wife, Ruth, is an artist, photographer, and illustrator. She has illustrated the following books for her husband: *Canoe Days* (2001); *Dogteam; My Life in Dog Years* (2009); *Puppies, Dogs, and Blue Northers: Reflections on Being Raised by a Pack of Sled Dogs* (2007); *The Tortilla Factory* (1995); *Woodsong* (1990); and *Worksong* (2000).

1979, things hit rock bottom. All Paulsen had in the world was $900 in cash and a car that was about to be repossessed. In an effort to live as cheaply as possible, Gary, Ruth, and Jim moved to a cabin outside of Bemidji, Minnesota. They had, as Paulsen said in an interview with Weidt, "no plumbing, no electricity, and no real prospects."

HIS FIRST SLED DOGS

Soon after, someone gave Paulsen a gift. Knowing that he had no means of transportation, a friend gave him a broken-down sled and four sled dogs—Storm, Yogi, Obeah, and Columbia. Paulsen had owned many dogs since his first, Snowball. Indeed, as he notes in his book *Woodsong* (1990), he believes that dogs are "mandatory for decent human life." But his first team of sled dogs was to change his life in ways he never anticipated.

Paulsen repaired the sled, and, as he had taught himself to sail, he taught himself to run a dog team. The sled dogs made it much easier for him to trap beaver. But they also helped him discover a new way of looking at the wilderness. Paulsen had spent much of his life outdoors, hunting and trapping, fishing, camping, and sailing. But working with the dogs brought him a new understanding of the natural world.

Paulsen pets one of his favorite sled dogs, Flax. Paulsen learned how to manage a sled dog team and came to respect the individuality of his dogs.

Just as his first dog, Snowball, had taught him new ways to observe the world around him, the sled dogs helped him see the beauty of the Minnesota woods in winter. "I would see a thing of beauty when running [the dogs]," he wrote in a memoir, *Winterdance*, "or many things, the pictures like frozen jewelry, and there would not be so much beauty when not running them. So I ran them because I wanted to see the beauty again, find the wonderful places they could take me."

As he spent more time with his dogs, his understanding of them deepened. He realized that they were not just working animals, but individuals. Some even had a sense of humor. Storm would tease Paulsen by hiding things from him—a glove liner, a roll of tape, a hat. Paulsen watched one day as Columbia played a joke on another dog, Olaf, by carefully placing a bone just beyond Olaf's reach. The dogs were also compassionate. One day Paulsen fell off the sled and broke his kneecap. He was in a bad situation: alone in the middle of a Minnesota winter, a long way from home, and unable to walk. The dogs were gone; sled dogs usually do not stop when their driver falls off. They are bred to run and love to run and will keep going. But this time, Paulsen's dogs didn't keep going. They came back for him, let him get on the sled, and brought him back home. Paulsen was amazed that the dogs had understood the situation, realized that he needed help, and figured out how to give it to him. He began to realize that he could learn from them.

"THE TRUE SANCTITY OF LIFE"

His experiences with his sled dogs changed one fundamental thing about Paulsen: he stopped hunting and trapping. He had spent much of his life up until that point killing animals for food and money. But after getting to know his dogs, Paulsen began to realize that human beings are not separate from and superior to animals. Killing anything—even killing to eat—became repulsive to him. "I began to have a real feeling for the true sanctity of life, began to understand that life is all the cosmos gives and that to remove it, from anything, is incorrect," he wrote in *Winterdance*.

Although he had stopped trapping animals, Paulsen continued to run his dogs over his old trap line. One night, Paulsen paused at the edge of a frozen lake where he always turned to go home. The dogs waited, expecting the command "haw" for a left turn. Instead, Paulsen told them, "gee"—the command for right. They took off down a frozen river with no plan other than to see what was around the next bend. Paulsen ran the dogs for four days. (He didn't think his wife would worry, but he was

While working with sled dogs, Paulsen acquired an understanding of the "true sanctity" of life and could no longer trap or kill animals.

wrong; Ruth thought he had died and called friends to search for his body.) For three days, Paulsen was accompanied by a small coyote that followed the dog team. A chickadee perched on the rim of his parka hood and stayed there for half a day, eating bits of meat from his fingers. Paulsen found a deer caught in an illegal snare, a steel cable around its neck, and set it free. As he wrote in *Winterdance*, he experienced "a fundamental change in how I perceived myself and the world. I did not elevate myself any longer, nor did I put the other aspects of nature down. It became, truly, we."

This wild, unplanned run with his dogs was later part of the inspiration for the novel *Dogsong* (1985). When a young Inuit boy named Russel Susskit cannot feel at home in his village, where snowmobiles whine outside his window and his father struggles with alcoholism, he takes a team of sled dogs out into the Alaskan wilderness on a run that, the village wise man tells him, will help him find his "song"—the truth about himself. Paulsen writes in *Dogsong* about Russel's run with the dogs in words that echo his own experience: "Into the sweeps, into the great places where the land runs to the sky and into the sky until there is no land and there is no sky … Into the white line of the ice-blink where the mother of wind lives to send down the white death of the northern storms … Russel went out where there is nothing, into the wide center of everything there is."

When Paulsen eventually returned home from the run, his wife saw him and came outside to meet him with a cup of hot soup in her hands. She asked him a question. Was he going to run the Iditarod? Naturally, the Alaskan wilderness drew him. Paulsen answered yes.

CHAPTER SIX

THE IDITAROD

The Iditarod (called The Last Great Race on Earth®) is a trail sled dog race that starts in Anchorage, a port city in south-central Alaska, and ends in Nome, on the western coast of Alaska, on Norton Sound of the Bering Sea. The Iditarod Trail Sled Dog Race covers a large portion of the state and crosses the Alaska Range along the way. It then runs to the Kuskokwim River, into the interior of the state, and then along the Yukon River, and west to the area of the artic tundra. Every other year, the route is changed somewhat. The route's finish line is in Nome. The race's route is about one thousand miles (1,609 km) long, and it is one of the most difficult and daunting races in the world. To become a musher in the race, a person must first qualify.

A musher and his dog sled wind their way through Rainy Pass of the Alaskan Range during the 1983 Iditarod. Paulsen trained long and hard for the 1983 race.

Although Paulsen had been working with dogs for some time, racing a dog team is different—in the same ways that riding a workhorse around a farm is different from running a thoroughbred in the Kentucky Derby. As usual, Paulsen plunged right in. He knew that he would need more dogs; you must have between seven and twenty dogs to run the Iditarod. He got them anywhere he could find them. Some he bought with money that he'd earned from writing and trapping, others were gifts from friends. He then set about making the dogs and himself into a racing team.

TRAINING

On one of his first attempts, he harnessed the dogs to an old bicycle because there was no snow on which to run the sled. The dogs were much more powerful than he expected, but they managed to pull the bike, with Paulsen on it, out of the driveway and onto the road without disaster. Everything seemed to be going well—until the dogs spotted a rabbit and dragged Paulsen, bicycle and all, into the woods in pursuit of it.

Later, Paulsen built a rig, a tricycle-like contraption that used the wheels from an old wheelbarrow. But he didn't know that you shouldn't harness more than four or five dogs to such a light load. He spent a good portion of the time being dragged out of the yard on his face, hanging onto the rig for dear life. Once, a packet of matches in his pocket ignited from the friction. Finally, Paulsen figured out that the dogs were too powerful for the light loads he had them pulling. He solved the problem by going to the dump and finding a car without an engine. It turned out that that the dogs could pull it easily.

Paulsen trained the dogs at night, when it was cooler. This schedule had one major drawback: skunks are nocturnal, and there are plenty of skunks in the Minnesota woods. One night, when Paulsen came home after encountering several skunks, his wife, Ruth, asked him to sleep in the kennel. Paulsen realized that this was actually an opportunity: if he lived with the dogs, he would begin to learn how they thought. "I read in the kennel, sewed in the kennel, slept, and even set up a bathroom and did that in the kennel," he wrote in *Winterdance*.

Paulsen was so busy training that he had no time for writing. That's what he told his editor, Richard Jackson of Bradbury Press, when Jackson called to ask what Paulsen was working on. When Paulsen confessed his financial difficulties, Jackson sent him a check, on the condition that Paulsen would send him whatever he wrote next.

GETTING MONEY FOR THE RACE

Training the dogs was only one of Paulsen's challenges. The Iditarod costs money. Paulsen not only had to pay the entry fees, but he also had to buy dogs and equipment and then transport the dogs, equipment, and himself to Alaska and back. Although his finances were in better shape than they had been a few years before, in 1979, Paulsen could never have afforded to do all this on his own. But his neighbors in the nearby town of Bemidji, Minnesota, pitched in. Wanting to help Paulsen achieve his dream, the townspeople donated gear, dogs, dog food, and cash. Picnics, potluck dinners, and dances were held to raise money, and businesses set up collection jars for donations. People would stop Paulsen on the street and hand him money, saying simply, "For the race."

THE RACE

At last, in 1983, Paulsen and the dogs were ready for Alaska. A friend who had donated a 1968 Chevy pickup truck decided to join Paulsen for the drive north. It took eight days, as Paulsen and his friend drove without stopping, pulling a trailer with twenty sled dogs who had to be let out every four hours.

At the banquet before the race began, according to *Winterdance*, Paulsen was unofficially voted "the least likely to get out of Anchorage." This turned out to be nearly accurate. At the last minute, Paulsen decided to switch lead dogs. The lead dog is the first in the team and directs the other dogs. Paulsen normally ran with a female dog named Cookie as his lead. She was astonishingly smart; as Paulsen writes in *My Life in Dog Years*, he considered her "a good friend, a kind of dogsister or dogmother to me." But Cookie had never experienced anything like the chaos of the start of the Iditarod, and Paulsen worried that she might panic. Instead, he put a dog named Wilson in front. Two blocks into the race, Wilson missed the first turn and took Paulsen and the rest of the dog team on an impromptu tour of downtown Anchorage. Shortly after this, just outside of Anchorage, Paulsen took a wrong turn. This not only took him sixty miles (96.5 km) out of his way, but led the twenty-seven teams behind him down the wrong path as well.

Eventually, Paulsen got back on the right track, and by the time he'd reached the first of the eighteen checkpoints that a racer, or musher, must pass, the experience of running the Iditarod was already starting to affect him. "I thought my whole life had changed," he wrote in *Winterdance*, "that my basic understanding of values had changed, that I wasn't

An Iditarod musher leads his sled dogs through the part of the 1983 trail that is near the Bering Sea. Paulsen finished forty-first in the Iditarod of 1983.

sure if I would ever recover, that I had seen god and he was a dog-man and that nothing, ever, would be the same for me again, and it was only the first true checkpoint of the race."

Before the race was over, Paulsen would experience hallucinations from sleep deprivation. He would see things that weren't there, including a naked woman, the ocean off the coast of California with surfers on the waves, and a man in a trench coat who rode on his sled and was talking about federal education grants. He would think seriously about quitting. He would be attacked by a moose and would watch that moose kill the lead dog of the sled behind him. He would run through a herd of caribou and see buffalo playing games on the ice of a frozen lake. He would watch a man kill one of his own dogs, deliberately kicking it to death. (The man was later disqualified from the race when Paulsen told what he had seen.) He would eat nineteen bowls of moose chili at a checkpoint. And he would run the dogs through wind so strong that it blew them, the sled, and Paulsen off the trail, driving sharp pieces of snow underneath his eyelids. He would run the dogs through weather so cold that his cheeks, fingers, and toes were frostbitten, and his matches would not strike.

He would lose track of time, running for hours across the vast, frozen beauty of the Alaskan wilderness, until modern life seemed unreal. "I have changed," he wrote in *Woodsong*, "moved back in time, have entered an altered state, a primitive state … We could run forever into this wind, across the short grass, run for all the time there has been and all the time there will be." When Paulsen at last reached the end of the race—he finished in forty-first place—he stopped, looking at the lights of Nome, and didn't want it to be over. Exhausted, filthy, starving, and half-frozen, all he wanted to do was turn the dogs around and run some more.

CHAPTER SEVEN

JUMP-STARTING A CAREER

Dancing Carl (1983), the book Paulsen had promised to Richard Jackson of Bradbury Press, was a story about a veteran of World War II who became emotionally damaged by his wartime experiences. Carl expresses his feelings by "dancing" at the local ice rink. Shortly after this, Paulsen wrote *Popcorn Days and Buttermilk Nights*, a book about Carley, a troubled teen who instead of being sent to a reform school, goes to rural Minnesota, to his uncle David's blacksmith forge, and learns to work steel and change his life. In 1984, came *Tracker*, based on Paulsen's boyhood experience of following a deer until he was close enough to touch it. The story is about thirteen-year-old John Bourne, who tracks a doe for two days and then discovers he cannot shoot her. Although he hunts to provide meat for his family, John ponders his role as a hunter and the significance of life and death while his grandfather is dying of cancer.

A GROWING REPUTATION

Paulsen's standing as a writer of young adult literature was growing. Although *School Library Journal* thought that *Dancing Carl* was "lacking in action," *The Horn Book Magazine* disagreed. "Filled with poetry and with life," a reviewer wrote, "the book is not only an insightful, beautifully written story for children, but for readers of any age." *Horn Book Magazine* also praised *Tracker*, saying, "The simple narrative expands effortlessly to address questions of spiritual growth without losing the immediacy of plot and characters." But it was Paulsen's next book, *Dogsong* (1985), that would add enormously to his reputation.

Written while he was training for his second Iditarod, *Dogsong* draws on Paulsen's experiences running dogs in Minnesota and Alaska. It is a poetic tribute to the connection between a boy and his dog team, between the past and the present, and between humanity and nature. It was widely praised for its combination of gritty adventure and beautiful writing. Richard Luzer, in a review in *School*

Library Journal, called it "unusual and moving" and "a remarkable book." *The Bulletin of the Center for Children's Books*, another review magazine, thought it was "slow-moving, but effective in its starkness and intensity." Ethel R. Twichell, in a review in *Horn Book,* said that Paulsen "succeeds in giving the brutal North a poetry of its own." *Dogsong* would become a Newbery Honor book, and its success finally brought Paulsen some financial security.

A SECOND IDITAROD AND *HATCHET*

In 1985, Paulsen made a second attempt at the Iditarod, but in the end, the weather was so bad that he couldn't see his team in front of him, and snow and ice blew into his eyes even though they were closed. Ultimately, as he recalls in *Guts*, the wind blew his dogs back on top of him in "a furry pile." Close to the end of the race, he got word to Nome that he needed to be picked up, and a small plane came to get him.

Two years later, in 1987, *Hatchet* was published, and something extraordinary happened. *Hatchet* is, in essence, a fairly simple story. Thirteen-year-old Brian Robeson is stranded by a plane crash in the Canadian wilderness and must survive on his own for fifty-four days until he is rescued. By paying attention to his surroundings and remembering facts and lessons from his earlier life, Paulsen wrote in *Hatchet*, that Brian masters the skills he needs to survive. He described the first time Brian caught a fish for food using an arrow: "He held the fish against the sky until it stopped wiggling, held it and looked to the sky and felt his throat tighten, swell, and fill with pride at what he had done."

A soldier relaxes and reads Paulsen's *Hatchet*, which was published in 1987 and won him his second Newbery Honor. It was the first book in the Brian Saga series.

Hatchet was more than a critical and popular success. It was a phenomenon. There have been many adventure and survival novels about protagonists who must struggle to live in the wilderness. But *Hatchet*, with its precise details based on Paulsen's own experiences, and its profound sense of respect for the natural world, touched a nerve with an astonishing number of readers. Although some reviewers criticized a subplot involving the divorce of Brian's parents, finding it contrived or undeveloped, they were otherwise universal in their praise. *The Bulletin of the Center for Children's Books* called *Hatchet* "deftly conceived and developed." "Paulsen emphasizes character growth through a careful balancing of specific details of survival with the protagonist's thoughts and emotions," wrote Barbara Chatton, a reviewer for *School Library Journal*.

Hatchet won Paulsen his second Newbery Honor. Suddenly, he was in demand as a speaker at schools and writer's conferences. He received countless letters from young readers (and some older ones as well) who longed to know what happened to Brian after he was rescued. In the end, these letters resulted in Paulsen writing four more novels about Brian and a memoir, *Guts*, describing events in Paulsen's own life that Brian's adventures are based on.

CHANGES

Paulsen's son, Jim, once said that *Hatchet* changed the family's life—the Paulsens were able to move from their cabin to a house near the city of Bemidji, and they actually had a washer and dryer. In an article ("Grumpy Old Man and the Sea: Adventures With Gary Paulsen") about Paulsen, Elizabeth Royte notes that Jim added, "We had no running toilets for most of my childhood."

A THIRD NEWBERY HONOR BOOK AND HEART PROBLEMS

Paulsen continued to write, publishing his third Newbery Honor book, *The Winter Room*, in 1989. He also continued to run dogs, planning for his third Iditarod. But his plans didn't work out right away. In 1990, he experienced chest pains and was told by a doctor that he had heart disease. It was not expected to be immediately fatal, and with a careful diet Paulsen could expect to live many more years. But his body couldn't take the stress of running dogs anymore. From the hospital where he had received the diagnosis, Paulsen called a friend who also ran dogs and told him to take everything—all the dogs, all the gear. By the time he got home from the hospital, the only thing left from what had been the focus of his life for nine years was his beloved lead dog, Cookie.

Cookie had arthritis and had retired from racing not long before Paulsen was diagnosed with heart disease. She moved from the kennel into the house, where she promptly ate one of Ruth Paulsen's cats. After coming home from the hospital, Paulsen spent most of his time at home. Cookie hardly left his side until her death.

At first, Paulsen thought that his diagnosis of heart disease meant the end of everything he loved. But he wasn't capable of giving up. Without the dogs, according to *Pilgrimage on a Steel Ride*, he found that Minnesota winters were "not as interesting." He decided to move south. First, he and Ruth tried Wyoming, living in a small cabin at the foot of the Bighorn Mountains. There he discovered that, although he couldn't race sled dogs anymore, he wasn't cut off from the wilderness after all. He bought two horses, Merry and Blackie, and began to explore the mountains. "Since diagnosed with heart disease I have seen cliff dwellings and deserts and mountains … have dodged bear and been bit by snakes … and seen sunsets and dawns that no man, ever, has seen before or will see again in the same way or place," he wrote in *Pilgrimage on a Steel Ride*.

NEW MEXICO AND MOTORCYCLES

Wyoming, as it turned out, wasn't far enough south. For a couple of years, Gary and Ruth moved back and forth between New Mexico and Minnesota. Eventually, in 1992, they settled in La Luz, New Mexico. There, Paulsen did something he'd wanted to do all his life: He bought a Harley-Davidson motorcycle. Then he took his new bike on a little ride—a twelve-day, nine thousand-mile (1,484-km)

La Luz is located in southern New Mexico and is situated in the eastern edge of the Tularosa Basin and to the west of the Sacramento Mountains. Gary Paulsen and his wife, Ruth, lived in La Luz in 1992.

trip from New Mexico to Alaska and back. In *Pilgrimage on a Steel Ride*, Paulsen said he found that "there is something very liberating about heart disease." He discovered that many of the things people think are important—"car payments, careers, lawyers, awards, families"—don't really matter. What matters is simply one thing: that you live life "the best way you know how."

A LOVE FOR THE SEA

While living in New Mexico, Paulsen rekindled his love for the sea. After his motorcycle trip to Alaska, Paulsen bought an old sailboat, *Felicity*, and sailed up and down the West Coast of North America. Off the Alaskan coast, as he wrote in *Caught by the Sea*, he sat at anchor while humpback whales fed nearby, "so close they could be touched, turning gently so that their flukes would not hit the boat, missing by inches, with killer whales mugging and fighting and playing around the boat in the clear, cold water."

Later, Paulsen bought a new boat, a catamaran, called *Ariel*. "Lord, she jumped out, seemed to leap forward with me," Paulsen remembered, in *Caught by the Sea*, about the first time he took *Ariel* to sea, "jumping from wave to wave, flat and fast and leaving little rooster tails in back of her two hulls like a speed boat." Paulsen made several trips on *Ariel* in the late 1990s, sailing to Hawaii, Samoa, Fiji, and back to Mexico. He hopes to sail around Cape Horn, the southern tip of South America, some day.

ANOTHER WRITING AWARD

Paulsen also continued to write. Few writers have been so prolific or have written in such a wide variety of styles. He has written both fiction and nonfiction, and his books include memoirs, survival stories, historical fiction, science fiction, picture books, and the Gary Paulsen World of Adventure and Culpepper Adventure series. Altogether he's published more than two hundred books and sees no end in sight.

In 1997, Gary Paulsen won the Margaret A. Edwards Award. Unlike many awards, which are given to a single book, the Edwards Award honors a writer's lifetime contribution to the field of young adult literature.

In 1998, *The Transall Saga* was published. In this science fiction fantasy/adventure story, a teenager named Mark goes into the future via a time warp, where he has to live a new life in a completely unfamiliar world. Mark encounters a bizarre primal society of the future, and he proves himself as a warrior and survivor.

Paulsen wrote two more books in Brian's saga, *Brian's Return* (1999) and *Brian's Hunt* (2003). In *Brian's Return*, Brian Robeson confronts life during high school while living in the city and decides he needs to go back to the quiet of the northern lakes and wilderness. Brian heads back to the Canadian woods in *Brian's Hunt*, where Brian discovers a wounded dog who soon becomes his companion. Brian becomes the hunter of a bear in this life and death adventure in which he uses his survival skills.

Another book, *How Angel Peterson Got His Name: And Other Outrageous Tales About Extreme Sports*, was published in 2003. Paulsen uses humor to relate "outrageous" and "extreme" stunts from the early days of extreme sports and Paulsen's nostalgia for his childhood. This account of thirteen-year-old boys who wrestle a bear at a carnival, hang glide, jump bicycles, skateboard, and bungee jump offered readers another look into some of Paulsen's autobiographical experiences.

A THIRD IDITAROD

Paulsen went back to racing the Iditarod in 2006, his third attempt to run dogs in the race.

On the website Iditarod.com, he said that he had missed sled dogs very much and was "making

Paulsen drives his sled dogs down Fourth Avenue in Anchorage at the start of the 2006 Iditarod. It was his third Iditarod, but Paulsen became injured and had to drop out.

a nostalgic run, non-competitive, simply running to finish." Unfortunately, his sled had run into a gate at the eighty-fifth-mile (137-km) mark, and he opened a vein and needed to drop out.

LOOKING AT THE NATURE OF WAR

In 2010, Paulsen considered war's savagery and cost to human life in *Woods Runner*. Samuel, a thirteen-year-old who spends days hunting in the woods for food for his family becomes involved in the American Revolution, in the colony of Pennsylvania. When his parents are taken prisoner by British soldiers, Samuel tries to track the trail, and in the meantime he encounters the harshness of the war and death as well as the goodness that people are capable of during tragic times.

A COLLABORATION

Paulsen and his son, Jim, worked together in writing a book for the first time with *Road Trip* in 2012. In the story, fourteen-year-old Ben goes on a journey with his father to rescue a border collie, Atticus. Other characters include a friend of Ben's, Theo, a car mechanic by the name of Gus, and a pretty waitress, Mia. The dog Atticus gives his own opinions about the trip, which complete the picture of the family dynamics and the characters' interactions.

In an interview with *Publishers Weekly* in 2012, Paulsen said that writing with his son was a great experience and fun. It was also a wonderful bonding experience, although he and his son had already been close. He also said he would enjoy writing another book with him in the future.

In 2015, Paulsen did just that. He and Jim published *Field Trip*, another story about Ben, who has been invited to try out for a hockey academy, his dad, and Atticus, the older and wiser border collie, Conor, a puppy, Brig, the house helper, and Ben's school mates, the twins Jacob and Charlotte. Ben's dad wants the group to travel to catch up to Ben's class, which is already on the school field trip. Ben, though, still secretly tries to make the tryout, and he and his companions end up having a comical and zany adventure.

Whether he's writing books, running dogs, sailing, or riding a motorcycle, Gary Paulsen doesn't stop easily. On his official website, Paulsen said, "Even after all these years, I am still amazed by the gifts that writing gives to me."

CHAPTER EIGHT

"TO SEEK A BEGINNING"

In book after book, Gary Paulsen writes about nature, wildlife, and the skills that are vital for survival. Paulsen's main characters find themselves facing dangerous situations, and readers keep turning the pages to discover if they will make it. Will Brian be rescued from the wilderness? Will Francis of *Mr. Tucket* make it to Oregon and find his family again? Paulsen's clean, direct style is well suited to his action-filled plots and easily pulls a reader in. "Stark and bare-boned," Betsy Hearne, a reviewer for *The Bulletin of the Center for Children's Books* described his prose, "without stylistic pretensions of any kind."

WRITING ABOUT HONESTY, REALITY, AND RESPECT

The challenges in Paulsen's books are never simply physical. *Children's Literature Review* has said that Paulsen "balances the characteristic action of his works by probing the thoughts and emotions of his characters as they move on inner journeys toward self-discovery." The emotional and mental aspects of survival give Paulsen's books depth. His characters endure plane crashes, storms at sea, poverty, war, and slavery; they also face isolation, the neglect or abuse of parents, and the deaths of loved ones. Forced to encounter difficulties that are both physical and psychological, they make it—they survive.

But Paulsen is not blindly optimistic; indeed, he is unflinchingly honest about life's difficult realities. The wilderness so many of his characters encounter may be a beautiful place, but life there is never easy. Paulsen doesn't shy away from telling his readers about his difficult childhood or his parents' alcoholism or his heart disease. He is uncompromising in showing the devastation of war and the brutality of slavery. "These matter-of-fact descriptions of human misery and senseless torture are probably unlike anything this age group has read or heard about," Susan L. Rogers, a reviewer for *School Library Journal* wrote of *Nightjohn*. With his sometimes

A Civil War–era photograph shows African Americans on a plantation in South Carolina. Paulsen researched slavery and its horrific effects in the United States before writing *Nightjohn* in 1993. The story was made into a movie in 1996.

brutal honesty, Paulsen is a writer that his readers can trust.

Paulsen's honesty is matched by a sharp eye for detail that makes his scenes vividly realistic. In *Hatchet*, for example, Brian spends six pages trying to light a fire without a match, each painstaking step described with such precision that readers feel as if they are there, watching Brian struggle. Paulsen's writing is so convincing, in fact, that after *Hatchet* was published, the National Geographic Society called him to ask if they could interview Brian. When Paulsen told them that the story was fiction, that he had made Brian up, they didn't believe him. It seemed impossible that there wasn't a "real Brian."

Paulsen is careful to foster his appetite and memory for the kind of detail that convinces readers. He takes trips alone so that he can pay careful attention to his surroundings; according to Rachel Bucholtz in "My Life's Work: Author," in *Boy's Life*, he describes his attention as "wolflike." In his historical novels, careful research takes the place of personal experience. It took Paulsen five years to do the research for the ninety-two-page novel *Nightjohn*.

Paulsen's love and respect for the natural world also brings readers to his work. "The lure of the wilderness is always a potent draw," Nancy Vasilakis, a reviewer for *The Horn Book Magazine*, wrote, "and Paulsen evokes its mysteries as well as anyone since Jack London." His characters come to understand the wilderness, and the lesson reverberates with force for his readers because Paulsen himself feels it so deeply. "While many adventure writers establish conflicts in their books that are resolved by a protagonist learning to subdue or conquer the natural world," Gary Salvner wrote in *Presenting Gary Paulsen*, "Paulsen's protagonists survive because they learn to respect it."

Toward the end of *Hatchet*, Brian recovers a rifle from the airplane's survival pack. But by this time, he feels so close to the wilderness that he is uncomfortable using the weapon. It will make his life much easier, and yet it will also separate him from his surroundings.

To respect the natural world means being open to the lessons it can teach. David Gale, in "The Maximum Expression of Being Human," in *School Library Journal*, noted that Paulsen has called the act of learning "the maximum expression of being human," and he himself has never stopped; he learned to hunt, sail, race a team of sled dogs, and write professionally. He learned from books, mentors, his sled dogs, and the world around him. His characters survive by gaining knowledge, knowledge about the wilderness and knowledge about themselves. Some of this knowledge they acquire by experience; some they find by listening to and learning from others. In *Nightjohn*, a twelve-year-old slave girl, Sarny, risks her life to learn to read and write to pass her knowledge on to others. Sarny's caretaker asks her teacher, Nightjohn, why Sarny and others should try to learn. "They have to be able to write," Nightjohn answers. "They have to read and write. We all have to read and write so we can write about this—what they doing to us. It has to be written."

PAULSEN'S WRITING ROUTINE

On Paulsen's official website, he describes his writing process. He said that he writes every day to give himself "balance and focus." He usually rises each morning at 4:30 a.m. and drinks a cup of tea. He uses a laptop or a pad of paper to write his stories. The location of the writing isn't important, he says, but what is important is "where the writing takes me." He has written books in his office, in a kennel for his dogs, on airplanes, and on his boat. Paulsen didn't start to write until he was twenty-six years old. He also noted that one key item in his office is a letter from one of his readers. It's framed, and he replied, "That means more to me than just about anything else."

PAULSEN'S COMMENTS ON WRITING

In 1997, when he won the Edwards Award, according to David Gale in *School Library Journal*, Paulsen knew he had many more books to write. At the time, he said he was probably "a hundred books behind." If Paulsen isn't writing a new book he's planning one, and if he isn't traveling he's planning a trip. This restless energy fills his writing. Paulsen's books sweep readers in from the first sentence and

Paulsen enjoys talking with young adult fans about his work and his life experiences. He finds young people inspiring. He said he writes daily and usually uses a laptop.

hurry them along with plots full of action. Reading his work, you get the feeling that this is not a man with time to waste. He has somewhere to go and is willing to take his readers with him—whether it's on a dogsled to Nome or a sea voyage to Cape Horn. In any case, the journey itself matters more than the destination because the journey is where you find new experiences. The journey is how you learn.

According to Paulsen's official website, he has tried numerous voices and styles in his writing. He said, "Sometimes the way to tell a story is even more important than the story itself." He also said that everything he does is "just a path to get [him] to that moment when [he] starts to work [to write]."

"To seek. Not to find, not to end, but to always seek a beginning," Paulsen wrote in *Pilgrimage on a Steel Ride* about his motorcycle trip to Alaska. The motorcycle trip had become "a pilgrimage only to seek" just as all the Iditarod races had been, and, for that matter, his entire life has been.

FACT SHEET

ON GARY PAULSEN

Birth date: May 17, 1939
Birthplace: Minneapolis, MN
Parents: Eunice (Moen) and Oscar Paulsen
Family heritage: Scandinavian
Current residences: A ranch in New Mexico and a sailboat on the Pacific Ocean
Age when he started writing: Twenty-six
First published work: With Raymond Friday Locke, *The Special War* (1966); first solo book *Some Bird's Don't Fly* (1968)
Early Work Experience: Trapper, farmer, worker at a satellite tracking station, actor, editor, and construction worker
Marital status: Married, to third wife Ruth Ellen Wright, an artist
Children: Lynn, Lance, and Jim
College attended: Bemidji College in Minnesota (1957–58) for engineering and University of Colorado (1976)
Interests: Camping, hiking, dog sledding, sailing, horseback riding, motorcycle riding
Pets: Dogs and horses
Interesting fact: Paulsen uses solar panels on his boat, which enable him to write on his laptop

FACT SHEET

ON GARY PAULSEN'S WORK

The Tucket Adventures

Mr. Tucket (1968)
Call Me Francis Tucket (1995)
Tucket's Ride (1997)
Tucket's Gold (1999)
Tucket's Home (2000)
Tucket's Travels: Francis Tucket's Adventures in the West, 1847–1849 (2003)

Plot summary: While on the Oregon Trail, Francis Tucket is kidnapped by Pawnee Indians, and he has many adventures. He meets a one-armed man, rescues children, and encounters robbers and rough storms on his trip home.

Brian's Saga

Hatchet (1987)

Plot summary: Brian Robeson spends fifty-four days in the Canadian wilderness after he survives a plane crash. He survives by using a hatchet that his mother had given him. Meanwhile, he also learns to survive his parents' divorce.

Awards received: American Library Association

Notable Children's Book, 1987; Booklist Editor's Choice citation, 1988; Newbery Honor Book, 1988; Dorothy Canfield Fisher Children's Book Award, 1989; Golden Archer Little Archer Awards, 1989; Georgia Children's Book Awards, 1991; Young Hoosier Book Awards, 1991, Iowa Children's Choice Award and Iowa Teen Award, 1990; William Allen White Children's Book Award, 1990; Maud Hart Lovelace Book Award, 1991; Flicker Tale Children's Book Award, 1990; Ohio Buckeye Children's Book Awards, 1991; Sequoyah Children and YA Book Awards, 1990; Virginia Young Readers Program, 1990

The River (1991)
Brian's Winter (1996)
Brian's Return (1999)
Brian's Hunt (2003)

Books about Alida

The Cookcamp (1991)

Plot summary: A little boy goes to live with his grandmother, who is a cook in a camp for workers building a road through the Canadian wilderness one summer during World War II. He learns to admire the crew and helps them to build the road.

Awards received: *School Library Journal* Best Book of the Year, 1991.

Alida's Song (1999)

The Quilt (2004)

Culpepper Adventures (Thirty titles beginning with *The Case of the Dirty Bird* [1992])
World of Adventure series (Eighteen titles beginning with *The Legend of Red Horse Cavern* [1994])

Other Novels
Winterkill (1976)
Tiltawhirl John (1977)
Foxman (1977)
Dancing Carl (1983)
Popcorn Days and Buttermilk Nights (1983)
Tracker (1984)
Dogsong (1985)
Plot summary: Russel takes his sled dogs on a tough race across the mountains, arctic tundra, and snow and ice. He learns to survive the wilderness and finds himself in the process.
Awards received: American Library Association Notable and Best Book, 1985; Parents' Choice Award, Parents' Choice Foundation, 1985; Newbery Honor Book, 1986; Children's Book of the Year Award, Child Study Association of America, 1986; and Volunteer Stated Book Award, 1989

Sentries (1986)
The Crossing (1987)
The Island (1988)
The Voyage of the Frog (1989)

The Winter Room (1989)
Plot summary: Eldon and his older brother, Wayne, live on a farm in northern Minnesota and spend their winters listening to their uncle David's stories about the old country, activities on the farm, and growing up.
Awards received: American Library Association Notable and Best Book, 1989; Newbery Honor Book, 1990

Canyons (1990)
The Night the White Deer Died (1990)
The Monument (1991)
The Haymeadow (1992)
Dogteam, illus. by Ruth Wright Paulsen (1993)
Harris and Me: A Summer Remembered (1993)
Plot summary: A city boy spends the summer with his aunt and uncle on their farm. His cousin Harris is a daredevil, and the two boys have many entertaining adventures in the country.
Awards received: American Library Association Best Book for Young Adults, 1993; New York Public Library, Children's Books: 100 Titles for Reading and Sharing, 1993

Nightjohn (1993)
The Car (1994)
The Tent (1995)
The Tortilla Factory, illus. by Ruth Wright Paulsen (1995)
The Rifle (1995)

Worksong, illustrated by Ruth Wright Paulsen (1997)
Sarny (1997)
The Schernoff Discoveries (1997)
The Transall Saga (1998)
Soldier's Heart (1998)
Canoe Days, illustrated by Ruth Wright Paulsen (1999)
The White Fox Chronicles (2000)
The Glass Café (2003)
Molly McGinty Has a Really Good Day (2004)
The Time Hackers (2005)
The Amazing Life of Birds: The Twenty-Day Puberty Journal of Duane Homer Leech (2006)
The Legend of Bass Reeves (2006)
Lawn Boy (2007)
Mudshark (2009)
Notes from the Dog (2009)

Woods Runner (2010)
Plot summary: During the Revolutionary War, Samuel hunts for food for his family in the woods of the colony of Pennsylvania. When he returns home, he finds the settlement has been burned and that his parents have been taken prisoner by British soldiers. Samuel tries to rescue them, and, in the process, he battles enemies, sees the horrors of war, and makes new friends.
Awards received: Nominee for the following: Oklahoma Sequoyah Children's Book Award, 2010; Florida Sunshine State Book Award, 2011 IRA Teachers' Choices, 2011; Rhode Island Teen Book Award, 2012; New York State Charlotte

Award, 2011; Kentucky Bluegrass Award, 2011; and South Carolina Children's Book Award, 2012. Winner of Parents' Choice Awards, Spring 2010 Fiction; the National Council for the Social Studies (NCSS) and Children's Book Council (CBC) Notable Children's Trade Books in the Field of Social Studies, 2011; YALSA Best Books for Young Adults, 2011, PEN Center USA Literary Award, 2011 Finalist United States; and Capitol Choices Noteworthy Audiobook, 2011.

Lawn Boy Returns (2010)
Masters of Disaster (2010)
Liar, Liar (2011)
Flat Broke (2011)
Paintings from the Cave (2011)
Crush (2012)
Road Trip, with Jim Paulsen (2013)
Field Trip, with Jim Paulsen (2015)

Nonfiction

Father Water, Mother Woods (1994)
Puppies, Dogs, and Blue Northers (1996)
My Life in Dog Years (1998)
Guts: The True Stories behind Hatchet *and the Brian Books* (2001)
Caught by the Sea: My Life on Boats (2001)
How Angel Peterson Got His Name: And Other Outrageous Tales About Extreme Sports (2003)
This Side of Wild (2015)

CRITICAL REVIEWS

Dogsong

"In this Newbery Honor book, 13-year-old Russel Susskit heeds the words of a wise Eskimo shaman and leaves his familiar village to begin a journey of self-discovery. The thoughtful plot is laced with physically profound scenes, realistic and savage, as the young man learns to survive in the cold white reality of the wilderness."—Deborah Zink Roffino, *The Mailbox*

Hatchet

"This Newbery Honor book is a dramatic, heart-stopping story of a boy who, following a plane crash in the Canadian wilderness, must learn to survive with only a hatchet and his own wits."—*Publishers Weekly*

"As he did in *Dogsong* ... Paulsen emphasizes character growth through a careful balancing of specific details of survival with the protagonist's thoughts and emotions."—*School Library Journal*

The Crossing

"Paulsen creates a stark, moving portrait of Mexican poverty and street life, of the desperation facing those who attempt "the crossing." Like the relationship between Robert and Manny, this book is brief and brutal but ends on a note of hope."—*School Library Journal*

Harris and Me

"Readers will experience hearts as large as farmers' appetites, humor as broad as the country landscape and adventures as wild as boyhood imaginations."—*Publishers Weekly*

"Truly one of Paulsen's best."—*Booklist*

"Paulsen has an excellent eye for the slightly off-beat details, from the hired hand who never seems to take a bath and the rooster who lies in ambush for human prey, to Buzzer the killer cat."—Charles R. Duke, *The ALAN Review*

Nightjohn

"Among the most powerful of Paulsen's works...this impeccably researched novel sheds light on cruel truths in American history as it traces the experiences of a 12-year-old slave girl in the 1850s. ...Convincingly written in dialect, this graphic depiction of slavery evokes shame for this country's forefathers and sorrow for the victims of their inhumanity."—*Publishers Weekly*

Brian's Hunt

"As always, Paulsen spins a fast-paced tale, characterized by a refusal either to soften the often gruesome details of life in the bush (here, partially eaten bodies, wounds riddled with fly eggs and worms) or to romanticize wildlife."—Elizabeth Ward, *Washington Post*

How Angel Peterson Got His Name: And Other Outrageous Tales About Extreme Sports

"These episodes will not only keep young readers, of both sexes, in stitches, they're made to order for reading aloud."—*Kirkus Reviews*

"Paulsen exhibits a wry sense of humor and storytelling ability as if he were sitting on a country porch with eager listeners at his knee." —*School Library Journal*

Woods Runner

"Paulsen takes readers inside the reality of this war [American Revolution], revealing the horrific conditions of the civilians who were taken prisoner. Between each chapter Paulsen includes information on various aspects of the war such as weapons, civilian deaths, orphans, and communication…His story will leave readers with a new sense of admiration for those who lost their lives in the creation of the nation."—*School Library Journal*

"Paulsen once again takes up the task of telling the story of a bygone era…he once again captures a moment in time and the people who lived it in a way that will educate and touch his readers. This is a fine historical novel and one that allows its readers to better appreciate all the costs that war exacts."—Greg M. Romaneck, *Children's Literature*

TIMELINE

1939 Gary Paulsen is born on May 17.
1944 Paulsen and his mother move to Chicago, Illinois.
1945 Paulsen and his mother join his father in the Philippines.
1949 The Paulsen family returns to the United States.
1957 Paulsen graduates from high school.
1958 Paulsen attends Bemidji College to study engineering but drops out after one year.
1959 Paulsen enlists in the army and studies electrical engineering and missile technology.
1962 Paulsen is discharged from the army. He goes to work for aerospace firms in California.
1965 Paulsen moves to Hollywood, California, and finds work as an editor at a men's magazine.
1966 Paulsen moves back to Minnesota. He writes and compiles the book about the Vietnam War *The Special War* with Raymond Friday Locke; he writes *Some Bird's Don't Fly*, a collection of funny essays about the missile industry.
1967 Paulsen moves to Taos, New Mexico.
1968 *Some Bird's Don't Fly* is published.
1969 His first young adult novel, *Mr. Tucket*, is published.
1971 Paulsen marries artist Ruth Ellen Wright, and they have a son, Jim.
1976 *Winterkill* is published.
1979 Paulsen and his family move back to Minnesota.
1983 Paulsen races in the Iditarod.

1985 Paulsen races in his second Iditarod.
1985 *Dogsong* is published.
1986 Paulsen's *Dogsong* is named a Newbery Honor book.
1987 *The Crossing* and *Hatchet* are published.
1988 *Hatchet* is named a Newbery Honor book.
1989 *The Winter Room* is published.
1990 Paulsen is diagnosed with heart disease. He gives up running dogs. *The Winter Room* wins a Newbery Honor.
1992 Paulsen moves to La Luz, New Mexico.
1993 Paulsen drives a motorcycle to Alaska.
1997 Paulsen wins the Margaret A. Edwards Award from the American Library Association.
1998 Paulsen's novel about the Civil War, *Soldier's Heart: Being the Story of the Enlistment and Due Service of the Boy Charley Goddard in the First Minnesota Volunteers*, is published. *The Transall Saga*, a work in science fiction is published.
2003 *Brian's Hunt*, the fifth book in the Brian saga, is published.
2006 Paulsen enters the Iditarod for the third time; he withdraws before finishing the race.
2012 Paulsen and his sculptor son, Jim, cowrite *Road Trip*.
2013 The New York Public Library lists *Hatchet* as one of the top one hundred children's books of the last one hundredf years.
2015 *Field Trip*, another collaboration with Paulsen's son, Jim, is published.

GLOSSARY

ALASKA RANGE A mountain range in southeastern Alaska. It contains Mount McKinley, also known as Denali, at 20,320 feet (6,194 meters) the highest mountain in North America.

ALLIES In World War II, the group of nations (including Canada, China, Great Britain, the Soviet Union, and the United States) who opposed the Axis powers (including Germany, Italy, and Japan). In 1945, the Allies were victorious.

BALOOT A duck egg that is left to rot in hot sand until the unhatched body of the duckling inside is partially rotted. Baloots are considered a delicacy in the Philippines.

CAPE HORN The southernmost tip of South America. To sail "around the Horn" means sailing between South America and Antarctica, through one of the stormiest regions in the world.

CATAMARAN A raftlike boat with two hulls (the body of the boat); regular boats have a single hull. Because of their light weight and low water resistance, catamarans are known for speed.

CORPSMAN A medic in the military, trained to perform first aid.

EXCHANGE The store on a military base.

FILIPINO A native of the Philippines.

GUERRILLA A member of a small band of fighters that works in secret, usually relying on hit-and-run tactics, ambushes, and sabotage.

HUK A shortened name for a member of the Hukbong Magpapalayang Bayan, or the People's Liberation Army, an armed group who tried to take over the government of the Philippines from 1949 to 1954.

IDITAROD An annual trail dogsled race in Alaska. The Iditarod starts in Anchorage and ends nearly one thousand miles (1,609 km) away, in Nome.

MAINSAIL The largest sail on a boat.

MEMOIR A writer's account of his or her own life. A memoir is usually shorter than an autobiography and often concentrates on a specific time or event rather than telling the story of the writer's entire life.

MENTOR Someone who guides or teaches.

NEWBERY MEDAL An award given every year to the most distinguished contribution to American children's literature. A number of Newbery Honor Awards (usually between two and four) is also given each year to books that the Newbery Committee considers to be of special merit.

SANCTITY The quality of being holy or sacred.

SHILL Someone who acts as an excited customer to entice others to pay for something; a promoter at a carnival sideshow.

TRAP LINE A series of traps to catch animals, set in an area that animals visit regularly.

American Library Association (ALA)
50 East Huron Street
Chicago, IL 60611-2795
(800) 545-2433
Website: http://www.ala.org
The ALA provides information, news, and resources for members, librarians, and all people who use libraries. It also supports intellectual freedom and lifelong learning.

Creative Writers Workshop
Department of Professional Studies and Special Programs
Emerson College
120 Boylston Street
Boston, MA 02116
(617) 824-8280
Website: http://www.emerson.edu/academics/professional-studies/programs-high-school-students/pre-college-studio-programs/creative-writers-workshop
This workshop is held annually during the summer at Emerson College and provides high school students the opportunity to develop writing skills and create works of fiction, nonfiction, poetry, and screenwriting.

Iditarod
Website: http://iditarod.com
The Iditarod Trail Race has volunteers who work to make the annual race happen and raise money

for the event. The website includes information on past races, the Iditarod's history, rules and regulations, route maps, and GPS tracking information and apps. The website also includes puzzles, scavenger hunts, and other games for students.

Gary Paulsen's Official Website
c/o Random House Kids
Penguin Random House
Random House Children's Books
1745 Broadway
New York, NY 10019
(212) 782-9000
Website: http://www.garypaulsen.com or http://www.randomhousekids.com
The Random House Kids page about Gary Paulsen includes a list of his books and biographical information.

Read.gov: One Book Programs
Library of Congress
101 Independence Avenue SE
Washington, DC 20540
(202) 707-5000
Website: http://www.read.gov
This government-sponsored website enables people to search for One Book programs and to seek resources for starting their own One Book projects. Information about U.S. book fairs and storytelling festivals is also offered.

Teen Ink
P.O. Box 30
Newton, MA 02461
(617) 964-6800
Website: http://www.teenink.com
A monthly print magazine, *Teen Ink*, its website, and book series are all written for teenagers, by teenagers.

Young Writers of Canada
Poetry Institute of Canada and Young Writers
P.O. Box 44169-PRPO Gorge
Victoria, BC V9A 7K1
Canada
(250) 519-0446
The Young Writers division of this organization holds annual poetry and short story contests for writers between the ages of seven and eighteen. Contests are free to enter and the winning entries are published in an anthology.

WEBSITES

Because of the changing nature of Internet links, Rosen Publishing has developed an online list of websites related to the subject of this book. This site is updated regularly. Please use this link to access the list:

http://www.rosenlinks.com/AAA/Paul

FOR FURTHER READING

Blasingame, James B. *Gary Paulsen* (Teen Reads: Student Companion to Young Adult Literature). Westport, CT: Greenwood Press, 2007.

Casey, Susan. *Women Heroes of the American Revolution: 20 Stories of Espionage, Sabotage, Defiance, and Rescue.* Chicago, IL: Chicago Review Press, 2015.

Chastain, Zachary. *Lost! Surviving in the Wilderness* (Survivors), Broomall, PA: Mason Crest, 2008.

Corbett, Sue. *Gary Paulsen.* New York, NY: Cavendish Square, 2013.

Michaels, Eric, and Steve McEntee. *Sled Dogs.* Portsmouth, NH: Heinemann, 2009.

Paterra, M. Elizabeth. *Gary Paulsen* (Who Wrote What?). Philadelphia, PA: Chelsea House Publishers, 2002.

Rajczak, Kristen. *Racing the Iditarod* (Thrill Seekers). Buffalo, NY: Gareth Stevens Publishing, 2014.

Rosen, Michael J. *My Dog! A Kids' Guide to Keeping a Happy and Healthy Pet.* New York, NY: Workman Publishing, 2011.

Wallenfeldt, Jeff, ed. *The American Revolutionary War and the War of 1812* (America at War). New York, NY: Britannica Educational Publishing and Rosen Educational Services, 2010.

William, Mike, Sr., and Lew Freedman. *Racing Toward Recovery: The Extraordinary Story of Alaska Musher Mike Williams Sr.* Portland, OR: Alaska Northwest Books, 2015.

BIBLIOGRAPHY

American Library Association. "YALSA: Margaret A. Edwards Award." 2000, retrieved January 1, 2002 (http://www.ala.org/yalsa/edwards/paulsen /html).

Bucholtz, Rachel. "My Life's Work: Author." *Boy's Life*, December 1995, p. 28. *The Bulletin of the Center for Children's Books*. Review of *Dogsong*. May 1985, p. 174.

Chatton, Barbara. Review of *Hatchet*. *School Library Journal*, December 1987, pp. 103–104.

Draper, Charlotte W. Review of *Tracker*. *The Horn Book Magazine*, June 1984, pp. 340–341.

Educational Book & Media Association. "EBMA's Top 100 Authors—Gary Paulsen." Retrieved May 4, 2015 (http://www.edupaperback.org /page-864529).

Gale, David. "The Maximum Expression of Being Human." *School Library Journal*, June 1997, p. 24.

Gale Group. *Major Authors and Illustrators for Children and Young Adults*. "Gary Paulsen." 2nd ed.

Hand, Dorcas. Review of *Dancing Carl*. *The Horn Book Magazine*, August 1983, pp. 446–447.

Hearne, Betsy. Review of *Nightjohn*. *The Bulletin of the Center for Children's Books*, February 1993, pp. 187–188.

Hedblad, Alan, ed. *Something About the Author*, vol. 111, pp. 136–145. Detroit, MI: Gale Group, Inc., 2000.

Iditarod.com. "Musher Details." Gary Paulsen, 2006 Iditarod Musher. Retrieved May 4, 2015 (http://

iditarod.com/race/2006/mushers/132-Gary-Paulsen/).

Keen Readers. "Gary Paulsen: 175 Books and Still Going Strong." Retrieved April 29, 2015 (http://www.keenreaders.org/gary-paulsen-175-books-and-still-going-strong).

Kirkus Children's and Young Adult Edition, review of *Hatchet*, August 1, 1987, pp. 1161–1162.

Kirkus Review. "*Field Trip*." Kirkusreviews.com. Posted May 12, 2015. Retrieved June 25, 2015 (https://www.kirkusreviews.com/book-reviews/gary-paulsen/field-trip/).

Kumar, Lia, ed. "Paulsen, Gary." *Something About the Author*. Vol. 189. Detroit, MI: Gale, 2009, pp140–150.

Lodge, Sally. "Q & A with Gary Paulsen and Jim Paulsen." *Publishers Weekly*. December 6, 2012. Retrieved May 4, 2015 (http://www.publishersweekly.com/pw/by-topic/authors/interviews/article/55019-q-a-with-gary-paulsen-and-jim-paulsen.html).

Luzer, Richard. Review of *Dogsong*. *School Library Journal*, April 1985, p. 98.

Marcus, Leonard S., ed. *Author Talk*. New York, NY: Simon & Schuster Books for Young Readers, 2000.

New York Public Library. "Author Chat with Gary Paulsen." Transcript from live chat July 9, 2003. Retrieved May 4, 2015 (http://www.nypl.org/author-chat-gary-paulsen).

Paulsen, Gary. *The Amazing Life of Birds (the Twenty-Day Puberty Journal of Duane Homer Leech).* New York, NY: Wendy Lamb Books, 2006.

Paulsen, Gary. *The Beet Fields: Memories of a Sixteenth Summer*. New York, NY: Delacorte Press, 2000.

Paulsen, Gary. *Brian's Hunt*. New York, NY: Wendy Lamb Books, 2003.

Paulsen, Gary. *Brian's Winter*. New York, NY: Laurel-Leaf Books, 1996.

Paulsen, Gary. *Caught by the Sea: My Life on Boats.* New York, NY: Delacorte Press, 2001.

Paulsen, Gary. *Crush: The Theory, Practice, and Destructive Properties of Love*. New York, NY: Wendy Lamb Books, 2012.

Paulsen, Gary. *Dogsong*. New York, NY: Bradbury Press, 1985.

Paulsen, Gary. *Eastern Sun, Winter Moon*. New York, NY: Harcourt Brace Jovanovich, 1993.

Paulsen, Gary. *Family Ties: The Theory, Practice, and Destructive Properties of Relatives.* New York, NY: Wendy Lamb Books, 2014.

Paulsen, Gary. *Father Water, Mother Woods: Essays on Fishing and Hunting in the North Woods.* New York: Delacorte Press, 1994.

Paulsen, Gary. *Flat Broke: The Theory, Practice, and Destructive Properties of Greed.* New York, NY: Wendy Lamb Books, 2011.

Paulsen, Gary. *Guts: The True Stories behind* Hatchet *and the Brian Books.* New York, NY: Delacorte Press, 2001.

Paulsen, Gary. *Hatchet*. New York, NY: Bradbury Press, 1987.

Paulsen, Gary. *Lawn Boy*. New York, NY: Wendy Lamb Books, 2007.

Paulsen, Gary. *Lawn Boy Returns*. New York, NY: Wendy Lamb Books, 2010.

Paulsen, Gary. *The Legend of Bass Reeves: Being the True and Fictional Account of the Most Valiant Marshal in the West*. New York, NY: Wendy Lamb Books, 2006.

Paulson, Gary. *Liar, Liar: The Theory, Practice, and Destructive Properties of Deception*. New York, NY: Wendy Lamb Books, 2011.

Paulsen, Gary. *Masters of Disaster*. New York, NY: Wendy Lamb Books, 2010.

Paulsen, Gary. *Molly McGinty Has a Really Good Day*. New York, NY: Wendy Lamb Books, 2004.

Paulsen, Gary. *Mudshark*. New York, NY: Wendy Lamb Books, 2009.

Paulsen, Gary. *My Life In Dog Years*. New York, NY: Delacorte Press, 1998.

Paulsen, Gary. *Nightjohn*. New York, NY: Delacorte Press, 1993.

Paulsen, Gary. *Notes from the Dog*. New York, NY: Wendy Lamb Books, 2009.

Paulsen, Gary. *Pilgrimage on a Steel Ride: A Memoir About Men and Motorcycles*. New York, NY: Harcourt Brace & Company, 1997.

Paulsen, Gary. *Puppies, Dogs, and Blue Northers: Reflections on Being Raised by a Pack of Sled*

Dogs. San Diego, CA: Harcourt Brace & Company, 1996.

Paulsen, Gary. *The Time Hackers*. New York, NY: Wendy Lamb Books, 2005.

Paulsen, Gary. *Vote: The Theory, Practice, and Destructive Properties of Politics*. New York, NY: Wendy Lamb Books, 2013.

Paulsen, Gary. *Winterdance: The Fine Madness of Running the Iditarod*. San Diego, CA: Harcourt Brace & Company, 1994.

Paulsen, Gary. *The Winter Room*. New York, NY: Orchard Books, 1989.

Paulsen, Gary. *Woods Runner*. New York, NY: Wendy Lamb Books, 2010.

Paulsen, Gary. *Woodsong*. New York, NY: Bradbury Press, 1990.

Random House Kids. "About Gary Paulsen." Retreived May 4, 2015 (http://www.randomhousekids.com/brand/gary-paulsen/).

Rogers, Susan L. Review of *Nightjohn*. *School Library Journal*, March 1993, p. 223.

Royte, Elizabeth. "Grumpy Old Man and the Sea: Adventures With Gary Paulsen." Outside Online. May 23, 2013. Retrieved May 4, 2015 (http://www.outsideonline.com/1919481/grumpy-old-man-and-sea-adventures-gary-paulsen).

Salvner, Gary M. *Presenting Gary Paulsen*. Twayne's United States Author Series, Young Adult Authors. New York, NY: Twayne Publishers, 1996.

Schmitz, James A. "Gary Paulsen: A Writer of His Time." *The ALAN Review*, Fall 1994. Retrieved May 4, 2015 (http://scholar.lib.vt.edu/ejournals/ALAN/fall94/Schmitz.html).

Sides, Anne Goodwin. "On the Road and Between the Pages, an Author Is Restless for Adventure." *New York Times*, August 26, 2006. Retrieved May 4, 2015 (http://www.nytimes.com/2006/08/26/books/26paul.html?pagewanted=all).

Trelease, Jim. "Author Profile: Gary Paulsen." Updated June 18, 2013. Retrieved May 4, 2015 (http://www.trelease-on-reading.com/paulsen.html).

Twichell, Ethel R. Review of *Dogsong. The Horn Book Magazine*, July/August 1985, pp. 456–457.

Vasilakis, Nancy. Review of *Woodsong. The Horn Book Magazine*, November/December 1990, p. 762.

Weidt, Maryann N. "Interview with Gary Paulsen." *Children's Literature Review*, Gerard J. Senick, editor. Vol. 19, pp. 167–178. Detroit, MI: Gale Research Inc.,1990.

INDEX

A

aerospace industry, time working in, 39, 40
Alcoholics Anonymous, 47
alcoholism, 18, 27, 33, 46, 53, 78
Alida's Song, 6
army
  father's time in, 10–11, 18
  Paulsen's time in, 37, 38–39, 41, 47

B

baloots, 22
Beet Fields, The, 6, 28
Beet Fields, The: Memories of a Sixteenth Summer, 32
Bemidji Teacher's College, 37
Brian's Hunt, 73
Brian's Return, 73
Building a New, Buying an Old, Remodeling a Used, Comprehensive Home and Shelter How-to-Do-It Book, 47

C

Canoe Days, 48
catamaran, 71
Caught by the Sea: My Life on Boats, 38, 41, 71–72
childhood, of Paulsen, 10–17
Cookcamp, The, 6, 13

D

Dancing Carl, 63, 64
dogs, relationship with, 23, 24
Dogsong, 6, 53, 64, 65
Dogteam, 48

E

Eastern Sun, Winter Moon, 15, 25
editor, working as a, 40–41

F

Family Ties: The Theory, Practice, and Destructive Properties of Relatives, 6

Father Water, Mother Woods, 27, 34, 35–36
Field Trip, 76
financial struggles, 46, 47, 48, 57

G

Guts, 35, 65, 67–68

H

Harris and Me, 6, 30
Hatchet, 6, 9, 16, 35, 36, 38, 65–67, 68, 79–81
How Angel Peterson Got His Name: And Other Outrageous Tales About Extreme Sports, 6, 8, 73
hunting, 8, 9, 34, 35, 36, 44, 49, 51, 64, 73, 75, 81

I

Iditarod, 8, 53, 54, 55–59, 61–62, 64, 65, 68, 73, 75, 84

M

Margaret A. Edwards Award, 72
memoirs, 6, 27, 33, 38, 41, 50, 67, 72
Minnesota, Paulsen's return to, 44–45
motorcycles, 70–71, 76, 84
Mr. Tucket, 44, 45
My Life in Dog Years, 24, 25, 48, 59

N

nature, connection to, 8, 9, 10, 34, 49, 53, 64, 77
Newbery Honor books, 6, 30, 65, 67, 68
Nightjohn, 8, 78, 80, 81

P

Paulsen, Eunice Moen (mother), 10–11, 12, 13, 14–15, 16, 17, 20, 23–24, 25
Paulsen, Jim (son), 47, 48, 75, 76
Paulsen, Oscar (father), 10–11, 12–13, 15, 17, 19–20, 21, 24, 25–26, 27, 28, 53
Paulsen, Ruth Ellen Wright (wife), 46, 47, 48, 51–52, 57, 69, 70

Philippines, 13
 during World War II, 18, 22
 journey to the, 14–17
 life in the, 18–26
Pilgrimage on a Steel Ride: A Memoir About Men and Motorcycles, 33, 69–70, 71, 84
Popcorn Days and Buttermilk, 63
Puppies, Dogs, and Blue Northers: Reflections on Being Raised by a Pack of Sled Dogs, 48

Q

Quilt, The, 6

R

Road Trip, 75

S

sailing, 8, 41–44, 49, 71, 72, 76, 81
school
 in Minnesota, 28, 35, 37
 in the Philippines, 20
sled dogs, 6, 8, 23, 58, 69, 75, 81
 first, 48–50, 51
 race, 54
Snowball, 23–26, 48, 50
Soldier's Heart, 8
Some Birds Don't Fly, 40, 44
Special War, The, 41

T

Tiltawhirl John, 6
Tortilla Factory, The, 48
Tracker, 63, 64
Transall Saga, The, 72–73

V

Voyage of the Frog, The, 6

W

Winterdance, 37, 50, 51, 52–53, 57, 59
Winterkill, 47
Winter Room, The, 6, 30, 68
Woodsong, 48–49, 62
Woods Runner, 8, 75
Worksong, 48
World War II, 11, 13, 18, 63

ABOUT THE AUTHORS

Denis E. McGuinness lives in Westchester County in New York. He has cowritten a book for young adults on the topic of descriptive writing.

Sarah L. Thomson is the author of *The Dragon's Son*, a retelling of the King Arthur legend for young adult readers, which received a starred review from *The Bulletin of the Center for Children's Books*. She has also written *Stars and Stripes: The Story of the American Flag*. After graduating from Oberlin College in Oberlin, Ohio, she moved to New York City to become an editor of children's books. She now concentrates on writing full-time, while residing in Portland, Maine.

PHOTO CREDITS

Cover, pp. 3, 7, 49, 74, 83 © AP Images; pp. 11, 29, 79 Library of Congress Prints and Photographs Division; p. 14 Frederic Lewis/ Archive Photos/Getty Images; p. 19 Photo © Tallandier/Bridgeman Images; p. 21 Fox Photos/Hulton Archive/Getty Images; p. 26 George Skadding/The LIFE Picture Collection/Getty Images; p. 31 Andrew Filer/ Wikimedia Commons/File: Carnegie library thief river falls.jpg; p. 34 Devin Koob/Shutterstock.com; p. 39 NASA; p. 42 Pung/Shutterstock. com; p. 45 Library of Congress Rare Book and Special Collections Division; p. 52 ventdusud/Shutterstock.com; pp. 55, 60 © Jeff Schultz/ AlaskaStock.com; p. 66 Nikola Solic/Reuters/Landov; p. 70 © Paul John Fearn/Alamy; cover, interior pages (book) © www.istockphoto. com/Andrzej Tokarski, (textured background) javarman/Shutterstock. com; interior pages (snow scene) vladimir salman/ Shutterstock.com

Designer: Nicole Russo; Editor: Kathy Kuhtz Campbell; Photo Researcher: Nicole DiMella